HOW TO FIND A HUSBAND
FOLLOWING GOD'S WILL

By Karen Elizabeth Totten

March 15, 203
Dear Lyia,
I wanted you
to have a
copy of my book.
I wrote it under
a per. name. Please
enjoy it
Karyl

1

Dedication

This book is dedicated to my Lord and Savior, the most
high, Jesus Christ,
To my wonderful husband Walter,
and to my dear son Garrett.

Prayer

In the name of the Father, the Son, and the Holy Spirit,

Dear Lord,

Please, shower this book with your blessings and infuse my words with your perfect wisdom so that every reader will feel your presence, guidance, and love as she travels on a journey here on earth. Thank you, Lord.

Amen.

Table of Contents

This is not a "get rich quick" book

More appropriately, this is not a "get a husband quick" book! In fact, it is not even a get a husband book. "Following God's Will" is the most important part of the title and purpose of this book. When we want something and pray for it, we must be willing to accept that God may not want it for us. That is why when we pray to God we need to follow the prayer with the words: "if it be your will." We must have faith that God will do what is best for us. And then we need to leave it in His hands. We may not understand how and when God allows something to happen, but we must have faith that there is, indeed, a master plan.

I am no expert on this, even though I've learned a lot researching and writing this book. I am a human being like you. I am a Christian on my earthly path and I am learning things as I go along. But I do want to share with you what I've learned in hope that it may help you on your path.

There are no quick and easy answers. Most things in life that are worthwhile take time. Many of us want the easy way. However, quick and easy schemes don't usually pan out.

It's like those diet ads that say you can eat all you want, sit on the couch and lose weight and firm up in just 10 days. How we all wish that would work!

Unfortunately, weight loss is not about miracles. To lose weight, you either have to eat less, or burn more calories. To find a husband, you need to pray, and wait. And you need to accept that you may never have a husband.

So now that you know that I do not have easy answers for you, why read this book?

I have been through this. I did not marry until the age of 43. I will share some stories and history of me and my friends. I hope you can learn from some of my lessons. I've also done a lot of thinking, praying, and living along the way, and I hope I can share some insight with you that can help you on your path. Every human being is special with a unique voice and perspective and can teach something to others. No one sees the world as I do and I believe that I have something meaningful and powerful to share with you.

I truly believe that the most important reason we are here on earth is to love, praise and serve the Lord, and to love and serve each other. I have a deep desire to help others, and I sincerely hope that something I have to say will be helpful to you and will assist you in being a stronger and healthier person.

I also believe that marriage is a sacrament given to us by God, and I want to support the institution of marriage. But I also want single people to know that they are not second-class citizens in God's kingdom because they are not married.

This is the advice I would have given to my sister if she had asked, and if I had known this at the time. The purpose of this book is for you to get a handle on who you are, what you want, why you want it, and who you want. There is a lot of bad advice out there. There are also lots of people hurting out here. And there are a whole lot of women out there looking for a husband.

So let's get started. If God is willing and the "creek don't rise", you will find a husband!

Having a personal relationship with God

When does a personal relationship with God begin?

It begins when we realize we need Him, admit that we are sinners, and in faith receive Jesus Christ as our Savior. God has always wanted to be close to everyone of us. Before original sin, Adam and Eve knew God on a personal level. They walked with Him in the Garden of Eden and talked directly to Him. Because of our sin, we became separated and disconnected from God.

Jesus gave us the most amazing gift, the opportunity to spend eternity with God if we trust and follow Him. "For the wages of sin is death, but the gift of God is eternal life in Christ Jesus our Lord." (Romans 6:23). God became human in the person of Jesus Christ to carry our sin, be killed, and rise again, proving His victory over sin and death. "Therefore, there is now no condemnation for those who are in Christ Jesus." (Romans 8:1). If we accept this gift, we become acceptable to God and can have a relationship with Him.

What does a personal relationship with God look like?

Whether we realize it or not, God is already part of our lives. "In him, we move, live and have our being." (Acts 18:26). It means that we become more aware of

God's presence in our daily lives. We should pray to Him, read the Bible, and meditate on His word in order to know Him better. We should pray for wisdom, and take our requests to Him. The Holy Spirit will act as our counselor. "If you love me, you will obey what I command. And I will ask the Father, and he will give you another Counselor to be with you forever—the Spirit of truth. The world cannot accept him, because it neither sees him nor knows him. But you know him, for he lives with you and will be in you." (John 14:15-17). The Holy Spirit lives in the hearts of believers and helps us fight against evil and temptations. The Holy Spirit also grants us the fruits of the Holy Spirit: love, joy, peace, patience, kindness, goodness, faithfulness, gentleness, and self-control (Galatians 5:22-23).

What does it mean to accept Jesus Christ as your Lord and personal savior?

Many people do not understand what this means. For a long time I didn't understand either. I repeated those words many times over the years not knowing what they meant, or what those words would mean to my life. It's a lot more than reciting words. Many can say "I accept the Lord as my savior." But if you really understand and mean those words, your whole life will change forever.

When I first said those words, I was at a Christian rock concert and was about fourteen years old. I said them again around the age of twenty-two. And I've said them a few times since then. However, in the past, it never felt like anything had changed. I guess I was expecting to say the words and like magic my life would instantly change. I would feel a difference, snap out of my old way of living, and everything would be easy from then on.

Now I know that when you accept Jesus as your savior it means that you accept him into your life and put him at the center of your being. You put him in charge of everything. You try to live the way he lived. You learn about him and try to do what he asks of you. You read the Bible. You go to church. You associate with other Christians. And you follow God's ten commandments. Most importantly, you learn to listen, so that you can hear God's words not only with your ears but also with your heart. That's what a personal relationship with God is all about.

Jesus was one of the most beloved people that has ever lived. He was born in a humble manger and came from a modest working family. He was also a man of great dignity and confidence. He didn't have any special breaks as child in education or employment, but he had the highest standards of human conduct that the world has ever seen. He made a huge impact on the world. Because of Jesus, millions of people now have a life of decency, honor and noble conduct.[1]

[1] Keller, W. Phillip, A Shepherd Looks at Psalm 23, Zondervan, Grand Rapids, MI 2007, pp. 23-26.

Many people say that they have accepted Jesus as their personal savior. They hope that by saying this they will somehow enjoy God's blessings and protection without paying any price. What is the price you pay? The price you pay is giving up your own foolish ways.

You cannot have it both ways. Either you belong to Jesus or you don't. You need to ask yourself some serious questions: Have I really accepted Him? Have I given my life to Him? Do you respect His authority and obey Him when he tells you what to do? Do you find purpose and contentment under His care?

If you can answer yes to these questions, you can proclaim "I have accepted Jesus as my personal Savior and shepherd. He is in charge of my life." And you will prosper and succeed no matter what life brings your way.[2]

I pray that you will welcome God into your life if you haven't already done so. The first step is to invite Him in!

---

[2] Ibid, p. 27.

How to follow God's will

I used to think that when you prayed for something, you were supposed to claim it and believe that it would happen. That is true, except that you must follow your request with, "if it is God's will." For example, "God, please give me a husband, if it is your will." We will not receive everything we ask for. God has a plan for all of us. We do not always know what that plan is, but we can rest assured that God knows His plan for us. If we listen carefully to what he tells us through his words and deeds, we will learn more about that plan.

Any righteous desires come from God. It is fine for us to want things. Wanting things can inspire us and can motivate us to work hard. All the great triumphs in the world such as discoveries, explorations, and inventions, have begun with a desire, a craving for more. God has created us and gave us a capacity to desire.

What we need to remember, though, is that it is not our desire alone that will determine the future. God has a plan, and we are part of the plan. Before you receive from God, you must delight in Him, commit your ways to him, trust him and rest in him.[3] We entrust our desires to the Lord and patiently trust that God will deliver to us if that's His will.[4]

---

[3] Psalm 37:1-8
[4] Dr. Charles Stanley, "The Desires of the Heart," 9/13/09.

If you really want a husband, I'm sure you've prayed for one before. Sometimes, when we think God isn't hearing us or isn't answering our prayers, He may be saying "no" to what we want. Who wants to hear that? Not many of us, so we think, *"He didn't hear me"*. Maybe it's not the right time for you to get married at this point in your life. Or maybe marriage isn't for you.

Let me tell you the story of a friend. She prayed for a husband. She found a husband. They got married and had a beautiful child, and, then, he left her and their baby. I can't tell you why that happened. And I hate that she had to suffer. Going through suffering can be a purifying experience. Gold is purified when it goes through fire.

That the trial of your faith, being much more precious than of gold that perisheth, though it be tried with fire, might be found unto praise and honor and glory at the appearing of Jesus Christ.

I Peter 1: 7

Your life as a Christian involves a process of refinement and purification from God.[5] God's goal is for you to be a holy, pure vessel that He can work through.[6] It's easy to have faith when everything is peachy. It's when times get tough that faith gets more difficult. That's when you realize your vulnerability and lack of

---

[5] Fire is the Test of Gold - There is No Perfection Without Refinement By Cathy Deaton http://ezinearticles.com/?Fire-is-the-Test-of-Gold---There-is-No-Perfection-Without-Refinement
[6] Ibid.

control.[7] Gold must go through fire in order to lose its impurities.[8] We all want to be pure gold, but we don't want to go through the trials that get us there. It's like a gospel song I love that says "Everybody wants to go to heaven, but nobody wants to die."

Like the song says: "You don't always get what you want – but you get what you need." The 23rd psalm says "The Lord is my shepherd, I shall not want." (Psalm 23:1). The good shepherd only wants its sheep to have what is best for them. It might not be what they want, but it will be what they need.

[7] Ibid.
[8] Ibid.

Waiting for the right time

To everything there is a season, and a time to every purpose under the heaven:
A time to be born, and a time to die;
A time to plant, and a time to pluck up that which is planted;
A time to kill, and a time to heal;
A time to break down, and a time to build up;
A time to weep, and a time to laugh;
A time to mourn, and a time to dance;
A time to cast away stones, and a time to gather stones together;
A time to embrace, and a time to refrain from embracing;
A time to get, and a time to lose;
A time to keep, and a time to cast away;
A time to rend, and a time to sew;
A time to keep silence, and a time to speak;
A time to love, and a time to hate;
a time of war, and a time of peace.

Ecclesiastes 3:1

There is a time for everything in our lives. Although we may think that we are in control and can plan each and every step, we are only fooling ourselves. The sooner we accept that we are not in control, the better off we will be. I believe that God is in control of my life. I also believe that I can act in accordance with God's plan or I can try to forge my own path apart from God. I can tell you from experience that going along with the all-powerful God is a much better way to go!

Therefore, you will need to be patient. Some of us are not naturally patient. I'm not. But you can practice improving your patience through prayer and experience. The first step is to accept that finding Mr. Right is not 100% within your control. The biggest part of the plan is God's will. Here is a Bible quote to help you wait:

Don't get tired of doing what is good. Don't get discouraged and give up, for we will reap a harvest of blessing at the appropriate time.

Galatians 6:9

What are you looking for?

Give me six hours to chop down a tree and I will spend the first four sharpening the axe.

Abraham Lincoln

Never underestimate the power of vision and preparation. First, you need to see the thing you want, then, you need to prepare for it. Only then is it possible for you to achieve it. Imagine searching for a needle in a haystack when 1) you don't know you are searching for a needle, and 2) you don't even know what a needle is? That's what some of us are doing. Looking for a husband and having no idea what marriage is, what we want in a marriage, and what kind of person we are looking for.

Let's start with marriage. What truth about marriage did God communicate to us?

Marriage is a sacrament.

A sacrament is a formal religious act or rite and one held to be instituted by Christ. God created man and woman and made them for each other to live and love each other in marriage. This marital union is part of the original divine plan and is for the good of the couple and the children that come from the marriage.

21

I believe that it was no coincidence that the first miracle Jesus performed took place at a wedding. The wedding was in Cana and the mother of Jesus was there. Jesus and his disciples were also invited. When the wine ran short, Mary told Jesus about it. Jesus turned water into wine. This was the beginning of his signs, revealed his glory, and when his disciples first started to believe in him. (John 2:1-12)

Marriage is permanent.

Since they are no longer two but one, let no one separate them, for God has joined them together.

Matthew 19:6

Marriage is a joining of two people into one. God does the joining and it is intended to be a joining forever. Needless to say, it is no slight or temporary undertaking.

Marriage is friendship.

The two of us have vowed friendship in God's name.

1 Samuel 20:42

Having a husband should be like having a best friend. My husband is my best friend. He doesn't love chick flicks but he will watch them with me! He is the person I share most things with. He is there for me and I am there for him. We enjoy being together. We care about each other and love each other as friends do.

Marriage is love.

Love one another deeply, from the heart.

1 Peter 1:22

Love is so important and central. God is love. Jesus is love. All that comes from God is good and based in love. Therefore, it is not surprising that marriage, a sacrament from God, would also be based in love. Without love, there is no marriage. I may get angry with my husband, and not like what he said or did, but I always love him.

Marriage is primary.

This explains why a man leaves his father and mother and is joined to his wife, and the two are united into one.

Genesis 2:24

23

Once two are married, everything else is becomes secondary. The husband and wife partnership is central and comes first. It is the first building block of our families and communities. It started with the first man and woman, Adam and Eve. From the marriage, children are born. When those children grow to adulthood, they too marry and form additional marital units with more children. And so on and so on. This has happened since the beginning of time and is as God intended.

Marriage is compatible, balanced and has a strong foundation.

Do not be yoked with those who are different, with unbelievers. For what partnership do righteousness and lawlessness have? Or what fellowship does light have with darkness? What accord has Christ with a liar? Or what has a believer in common with an unbeliever?

2 Corinthians 6:14-15

A marriage must rest on solid bedrock. We must join ourselves with someone who believes as we do. Inherent in this is the concept of compatibility. But I am not talking about a superficial compatibility like whether you like your toilet paper roll to go under or over. I mean a deep spiritual and moral compatibility about how we view God, ourselves, and the world.

Although I am a Catholic and my husband is not, we both share a deep belief in God and God's ultimate power over us and our lives and a willingness to follow God's will. I believe this kind of compatibility is extremely important in a marriage and helps ensure that it will endure the test of time.

Why do you want to get married?

When I ask "*why you want to get married*", I mean, "Why do YOU want to get married". What does marriage mean to you? To help you answer this question you will need to take a look at a few things, including your family history. A dear friend of mine recently went through a divorce and is starting the annulment process with the Catholic Church. That process has involved her looking closely at her family background, her parents' marriage, her relationship with each parent, past emotional and physical illnesses, her school years, personality and character, her spouse's background, her courtship and engagement and so on. How great would it be to go through this type of exercise before you even start to look for a spouse?

Marriage means different things to different people and is influenced by your age, culture, religion, ethnic background, class, etc. It makes sense to study marriage as an institution and study what marriage has meant to you throughout your life. Who were your teachers? What did they tell you? What did you believe marriage to be? What things did you witness related to marriage?

I, like many girls, had a fairly tale notion of marriage. Although in my personal life I had been impacted by divorce (my parents and grandparents) I believed that my knight would rescue me from this and other dangers. I did not have a very practical idea of marriage for myself. I also thought it would just happen and required no work on my part. I would just find the right person, we would get married, and we would live happily ever after.

Exercise[9] - Envisioning Your Marriage

Close your eyes and imagine your dream marriage. Answer the following questions based on how you would like your ideal marriage to be.

A. Your Courtship or Engagement Period
   a. How will you meet? Describe your dating habits.
   b. How do you get along together? How affectionate are you together and what part does sex play in your relationship?
   c. How does the subject of marriage come up in your conversations?
   d. Is there a formal engagement? How long will it last?
   e. How do you each feel about having children?
   f. What do you each believe about divorce?

---

[9] This exercise is taken in part from the Archdiocese of Washington, <u>A Guideline for Writing the Story of Your Marriage</u>, revised June 2005.

g. What parts will you each play in wedding preparations?
h. How will each one of your families view the marriage? How about your friends and his friends?

B. The Wedding Day
    a. How will you feel:
        i. As you dress for the wedding?
        ii. At the Church?
        iii. At the reception?

C. The Honeymoon
    a. Will you go on a honeymoon? How will you feel about it?
    b. How will you each feel about sex while on the honeymoon?

D. Your Married Life Together
    a. Describe your mutual love, affection, and sexuality.
    b. What is the attitude toward work and responsibility?

Remember, if you can see it, and you can believe it, you can achieve it. If it's God's will, of course!

Exercise – Looking at the real life marriages you know

- Take a look at the marriages in your life. What do you think makes a good or bad marriage?
- Focus on the good marriages. Talk to your family and friends about how they found each other, and why they think their marriages works.
- Look for and at patterns. One of the oldest marriages in my family is the marriage of my dear Aunt and Uncle. They have been married over 50 years. My Aunt's parents were also married over 50 years. My Aunt's son and his wife have been married over 30 years. They have a daughter who has been married 4 years in what appears to be a strong and healthy marriage. I don't believe it is a coincidence that that family has 4 generations of good marriages. Divorce also repeats itself. What are the patterns in your family? How might you work on breaking the negative patterns?

Right and wrong reasons to want a husband

RIGHT	WRONG
Completeness	Desperation
The Bible	Jealousy
Sacrament	Impatience
Partnership	Incompetence
Love	Appearance
Companionship	Lust
Security	Money
Prayer	External Pressure
Wholeness	Loneliness
Friendship	Status

How do you feel about yourself?

Have you heard that saying that unless you love yourself you cannot ever truly love anyone else? I used to hate that because I didn't love myself and it was an obstacle to my finding love with someone else. Besides, I didn't believe it. Although I used to be self-destructive, I have always been a very loving person towards others. Therefore, I thought I disproved the theory.

Self-esteem and self-worth affect how you will be with another person. Marriage is two becoming one. If one part of the mix is self-loathing, the couple will suffer.

What to do? Don't fret. It's time to do some work on you. First of all, be easier on yourself. Pat yourself on the back for making it this far and for always doing the best you could. Life is hard. Also recognize that self-improvement is a process and is gradual. Start loving yourself a little bit more each day.

The biggest part of learning to love myself involved turning to God. If God made me, I must be special. If God made me, I must be deserving. If God made me, how dare I mistreat myself! Seeing yourself as a child of God is an excellent first step in seeing yourself connected to God and others, of seeing yourself as a beautiful person. Seeing yourself as a child of God lets you feel God's love and allows you to love God through loving yourself. Imagine a dear friend giving you a precious gift. Would you leave it out in the rain? Would you leave it where it could get stolen? You would probably take care of it and cherish it. God is the ultimate dear friend and your life was a gift from God. Take care of that gift. Take care of yourself! Cherish yourself. Get out of yourself and really see who you are, a child of God!

Exercise[10] - Looking at your past

A. Your Family Background
   a. What were your parents like and how did they get along?
   b. Which parent was dominant in your family?
   c. How did you get along with each parent?
   d. Did you have any emotional or serious physical illnesses?

B. Your School Years
   a. How did you do in school? How did you get along with students and teachers?
   b. What were your attitudes about sex, drugs, alcohol and breaking the law?
   c. Describe your dating habits: when did you start dating, how frequently?

C. Your Personality and Character
   a. Briefly describe your character, its strong and weak points. Please consider the

---

[10] This exercise is taken in part from the Archdiocese of Washington, A Guideline for Writing the Story of Your Marriage, revised June 2005.

following: unusual fears in childhood, selfishness, self-confidence, suspiciousness, misinterpreting others' words or actions, nervousness, moodiness, inclination towards anger, stubbornness, ability to make and maintain friends, inappropriate silliness or outbreaks of crying, weakness of character such as lying or stealing.

Do you have issues?

Don't we all? What I'm getting at here are serious issues that you will need to sort through and examine, perhaps with the help of a priest, minister, or trained professional. These issues may include abandonment, physical or emotional abuse, sexual assault, failure to commit, addictions, and promiscuity. If you have a history of these things, or if you have a pattern of dating people with these issues, please stop now and get yourself some help.   It may be that now is not the time to be looking for a husband. Take this time to help yourself, change your behavior, heal and begin a new life.

Getting your house in order

Be the best you can be! Be fully satisfied with yourself. What if you never find a husband? How can you make the best life for yourself assuming there will never be a Mr. Right? What would your perfect life look like without a husband? Go ahead and make that happen. If it is not in God's plan for you to marry, imagine how meaningful your life can still be! If you do find a husband, look how much you will have to offer and the great launching pad you will have created! It's the best kind of proposition: win-win!

Take this time to work on yourself. Make yourself even more fabulous.

Beauty

Beauty is only skin deep. What is beautiful in the eyes of God? God sees the beauty on the inside. When the prophet Samuel looked at Jesse's sons in search of the next king of Israel, he was impressed with Eliab's appearance. God said to Samuel, "Do not consider his appearance or his height, for I have rejected him. The LORD does not look at the things man looks at. Man looks at the outward appearance, but the LORD looks at the heart" (I Samuel 16:7).

The Beatitudes also show us some of God's standards of beauty. Humility, righteousness, mercy, being pure of heart, and peacefulness are all qualities of inner beauty. The twelve fruits of the Holy Spirit also show what God finds beautiful.

The Twelve Fruits of the Holy Spirit

1. Charity
2. Joy
3. Peace
4. Patience
5. Kindness
6. Goodness
7. Generosity
8. Gentleness
9. Faithfulness
10. Modesty
11. Self-Control
12. Chastity

Conversely, there are the things that God finds ugly. There are things the Lord hates, for example: arrogance, lying, killing the innocent, scheming, evil, giving false witness, and sowing discord among brothers (Proverbs 6:16-19). Other things that are ugly in God's sight are the Seven Capital Sins.

The Seven Capital Sins

1. Pride
2. Covetousness
3. Lust
4. Anger
5. Gluttony
6. Envy
7. Sloth

The good news is that each of us can become beautiful in the eyes of God. Jesus can make us beautiful by forgiving us and teaching us how to live. Luckily, we have things to guide us. We have our own relationship with God, the word of God in the Bible, and our churches to help guide us.

Purity and Modesty

I cannot say enough about purity. We live in a world and time that is so saturated with the inappropriate use and abuse of sexuality. Women reveal so much of their bodies that should remain private and covered. Sexuality is a beautiful thing but it is not to be shared with everyone. Sex is thrown at us 24 hours a day. We as women are supposed to exude sexiness in our dress and demeanor.

I was recently in the airport and saw a group of teenaged Mormon girls. I cannot tell you how refreshing it was to see their faces with no make-up, their hair natural, and wearing long skirts with blouses buttoned to the neck. It was so appropriate, wholesome and beautiful. You can find clothing stores on-line that sell modest clothing for women. Check them out. And if you are not ready for the Amish look, at least take a look at how you dress and ask God if that is what He wants for you.

When I was confirmed in the Catholic faith, I had to choose a Saint as my confirmation Saint. I chose St. Rose of Lima because she stood for purity and modesty. Purity and modesty are virtues that appear to be long forgotten. St. Rose was so concerned that those around her were only interested in her appearance that she rubbed pepper on her face until her skin was blistered, dressed in rough clothing, and cut off her hair to prevent anyone from being tempted by her and so that she would not succumb to vanity. The next time you are not happy with how you look, how much you weigh, or how your hair looks, please remember St. Rose and her modesty.

Make sure you are acting like a lady. Acting like a lady means you behave using the manners your grandmother would be proud of. Men should treat you with the respect they would show their mother or sister.

All sin carries serious consequences. Sexual sin is no different in that regard. God wants us to live in purity of mind and body. Thessalonians 4:3-5 says "Abstain from sexual immorality; that each of you knows how to possess his own vessel in sanctification and honor, not in lustful passion." Your body does not belong to you. It is the temple of God. We must use our bodies to glorify the Lord.

Sexuality is a celebration of a total self-giving in love that enhances that love. Pleasure is a part of it but not the purpose. Sexuality is also for populating the earth. It is reserved for marriage. The devil wants us to believe that sexual promiscuity is normal. Sexual promiscuity is not normal, and it is not healthy for our bodies, minds or spirits. Here are some of the consequences of sexual sin: guilt, anxiety, low self-esteem, emptiness, anger, depression, dishonesty, disease, and abortion.

The good news is that sexual sin, like other sins, can be forgiven. You will need to confess your sins, ask God to forgive you, sincerely repent, and put your sinful behavior behind you. If you suffer from sexual addictions please seek a professional or spiritual help. Married people can prevent sexual sin by meeting each others needs faithfully. If you are single, you can prevent sexual sin by having Godly friendships that promote holiness and accountability, hanging around with groups of friends, and remaining celibate.[11]

Good Works

Don't forget to give of yourself to your family, friends, church and community. Give to the poor. Help children. Give to blood drives or food drives. Help a

---

[11] In Touch Ministries, Life Principles Notes, Landmines in the Path of the Believer, Part 5: The Landmine of Sexual Sins.

friend with babysitting. Make food for the grieving.
Visit the sick at the hospital. Send cards to people who
are hurting. There are so many things we can do to help
each other. We all have so many gifts. Figure out what
your gifts are and use them to help someone else or to
just brighten their day. Kind words, a warm smile, or a
hug can help you grow in love. Although they are free
for you to give, they are priceless in the lives of others.
And you wouldn't believe the joy you can get from doing
good works for others.

*"Teacher, which is the greatest commandment in the
Law?" Jesus replied: "Love the Lord your God with all
your heart and with all your soul and with all your mind.
This is the first and greatest commandment. And the
second is like it: Love your neighbor as yourself. All the
Law and the Prophets hang on these two
commandments."*

Matthew 22:36-40

Faith needs to be backed up by good works.

James 2:14-18

Health

How wondrous the body is. It thinks, feels and
imagines. It breathes. It can run! Marvel at it. What a
gift. Love it. Cherish it. Be thankful for it. Thank God
for it. Take care of it. Our bodies are the temple of God.
And we are the children of God. That means eating

healthy foods, exercising, getting enough rest and all the things that will maintain health in our bodies. We should be truly grateful to have bodies and thank God for them.

Know ye not that ye are the temple of God, and that the Spirit of God dwelleth in you? If any man defile the temple of God, him shall God destroy; for the temple of God is holy, which temple ye are.

1 Corinthians 3:17

Spirituality

What is your relationship with God like? Do you go to church? Do you have a religion? How close is your relationship with God? Wherever you are now, you can work towards a more meaningful and close relationship with God. You can start by accepting Jesus Christ as your personal savior. Accept that He died for your sins. That He loves you and will be with you forever and will live inside of you. Embrace God! Give Him a chance in your life. He will do wonders.

On a personal note, I don't know what I would do without God or where I would be without him. I give him credit for all that I am, all that I have, and all the tribulations I have survived. I thank him for all the blessings he has bestowed upon me and I thank him for sending his only Son to suffer and die a painful and humiliating death for me.

Abundance and Financial Stewardship

God wants us to have a life in abundance.

*Happy are those who do not follow the counsel of the
wicked, nor go the way of sinners, nor sit in company of
scoffers.*
*Rather, the law of the Lord is their joy; God's law they
study day and night.*
*They are like a tree planted near streams of water that
yields its fruit in season; its leaves never wither;
whatever they do prospers.*

Psalms 1:1-3

Just as a parent rejoices when their child is blessed, so is
it with God. We are his children and he is happy when
we are faithful. Abundance has many different forms; it
is not just money. It is your health, your body, your
relationships, your vocation, your thoughts, and your
creativity. Abundance also includes sharing what you
have with others.

*Here, then, I have today set before you life and
prosperity, death and doom.*
*If you obey the commandments of the Lord, your God,
which I enjoin on you today, loving him, and walking in
his ways, and keeping his commandments, statutes and
decrees, you will live and grow numerous, and the Lord,
your God, will bless you in the land you are entering to
occupy.*

Deuteronomy 30:15

On earth we need money to survive. God's promise to us for prosperity comes with a condition that we put God first in all things and that we use our prosperity to bless others.[12]

Command them to do good, to be rich in good deeds, and to be generous and willing to share.

1 Timothy 6:18

The Bible teaches us:

And my God will meet all your needs according to his glorious riches in Christ Jesus.

Philippians 4:19

Notice that it says that God will meet all your needs, not your wants. It is very important that you put your finances in order. One way to do this is to put God in charge of your finances. God should be first in all aspects of your life. Why should your finances be any different? God provides for us and in turn we have the responsibility to be good stewards of the resources given to us: the earth, our skills, and our money.[13]

---

[12] Michelle Singletary, The Power to Prosper: 21 Days to Financial Freedom (Grand Rapids, MI: Zondervan, 2010), p. 34.

[13] An excellent book on this subject is Michelle Singletary's The Power to Prosper. It was a life-changing book for me and many others. In a nutshell, it is a God-centered, and biblically rooted exercise in improving your financial life. I highly recommend it!

Tithing

Tithing is a concept as old as the Old Testament. The tithe required Israelites to give 10 percent of everything they earned to the Temple. (Leviticus 27:30). In the New Testament, Paul states that believers should set aside a portion of their income for support of the Church. (1 Corinthians 16:1-2). Every Christian should pray and seek God's wisdom with regard to tithing. (James 1:5). "Each person should give what he has decided in his heart to give, not reluctantly or under compulsion, for God loves a cheerful giver" (2 Corinthians 9:7). Please give lovingly to your church and support it with your prayer, time and energy.

Education

The very first book of Proverbs, also known as the book of wisdom, speaks of learning.

The proverbs of Solomon, the son of David, King of Israel: That men may appreciate wisdom and discipline, may understand words of intelligence; may receive training in wise conduct, in what is right, just and honest; That resourcefulness may be imparted to the simple, to the young man knowledge and discretion.
A wise man by hearing them will advance
In learning, an intelligent man will gain some guidance, that he may comprehend proverb and parable,` the words of the wise and their riddles.

The fear of the Lord is the beginning of knowledge; wisdom and instruction fools despise.

This passage puts knowledge and learning into perspective. First and foremost, knowledge is the fear of the Lord, following God's will and obeying his laws. The Bible is a rich resource that can reveal words of wisdom about the difficult situations we face every day. In addition, prayer can help us come to a deeper understanding of the Word of God.

It is important for each of us to keep learning and growing as God asks us to do. We should learn about God and ourselves. We should also educate ourselves to improve ourselves in whatever work we do.

Being yourself – being honest

Christ said that He is the Way, the Truth, and the Life. Being honest is about following in God's footsteps. If you want to become closer to God, you will need to focus on honesty.

Honesty guides good people; dishonesty destroys treacherous people.

Proverbs 11:3

When you are looking for a husband, be honest about who you are. Be honest about your past. Be honest about your hair color. Be honest about your weight. Be honest in all things big and small. You need to do this on your walk with God, and if you want to begin any relationship with a foundation of truth and honesty, you will need to do your part in bringing honesty to the table.

Besides, that way you are more likely to find someone who loves you for you. My husband doesn't like when I alter my hair or wear makeup. He likes me the way I am. It's nice to be encouraged to be who we already are. It's so much easier and honest to be ourselves!

What kinds of people do you attract?

Notice that I use active language here: what kinds of people do YOU attract into your life. You may not even be aware of it but your thoughts, your behavior, your mannerisms, the way you dress, where you go, and who you hang around with are all giving signals to the worlds. They are transmitting a message about who you are and what you want. Take a look at your self from the outside in. What kind of person do you think you are? Studious? A party girl? Someone who cares about herself? Some one who respects herself?

Sometimes it is hard to really see yourself as you are. It may be necessary to look at the effects of your behavior instead. Who is interested in you? Are you attracting superficial people that are only looking for a good time? People who are not interested in commitment? Are you hanging out in bars and dressing provocatively? If you are not attracting the people you want into your life, maybe you need to make some changes.

Speaking of attracting people into your life, let's talk about friends. When I became a Christian, I had to take stock of my life and some of my friends had to go. It's not that I don't still care about them, but there were people who were not good for me and I had to let them go.

You have to be selective about your friendships.
Friendship is not a charity, it should be reciprocal.

God's plan for marriage

Marriage matters! It is a private relationship with a spiritual and public significance.[14] Marriage is between a man and a woman to give children a structure in which they are created and nurtured, benefiting from the unique gifts of both a father and a mother.[15] Marriage is the foundation of the family and the building block of society. Men and women complement each other physically, psychologically and emotionally.[16]

We can learn much about God's plan for marriage through a look at 'Theology of the Body.' 'Theology of the Body' was Pope John Paul II's integrated vision of the human person, body, soul, and spirit.[17] His theory was that the physical human body has a specific meaning and reveals answers about the fundamental questions we have about ourselves such as the following[18]:

- What is the meaning of life?
- Why were we created male and female?
- What does marriage tell us about God and his plan for our lives?

---

[14] Marriage Matters, Archdiocese of Washington, www.MarriageMattersDC.org.
[15] Ibid.
[16] Ibid.
[17] http://www.theologyofthebody.net/; Christopher West, 09/26/09
[18] Ibid.

Pope John Paul II asked us not to view the body as an object of pleasure.[19] He encourages us to respect the gift of our sexuality and challenges us to live in a way that is worthy of our great dignity as human persons.[20] His theology is not just for young adults or married couples, but for all ages since it sums up the true meaning of the human person.[21]

As we begin to look at marriage, let us start with sexual morality. The most fundamental way to look at sexual morality is in the context of love and responsibility.[22] What we will be looking at is a person and their sexual desires, the love that grows on this basis between and a man and a woman, and the virtue of purity as essential to that love, and finally the issue of marriage and vocation.[23]

A primary and important concept is that people are not things and they are different from animals.[24] Human beings are rational, and have a spiritual character.[25] Love is the opposite of using the other person as an object to satisfy our desires.[26] People are not objects nor were they intended by God to be used as objects.[27] Love is where two people consciously choose

---

[19] Ibid.
[20] Ibid.
[21] Ibid.
[22] Karol Wojtyla (Pope John Paul II), Love and Responsibility, transl. by H.T. Willetts, Ignatius Press, San Francisco, CA, 1981, p. 16.
[23] Ibid.
[24] Ibid, p. 21.
[25] Ibid, p. 22.
[26] Ibid, p. 28.
[27] Ibid.

a common good to which both subordinate themselves.[28]
Love is not ready-made, but is something that people
need to live up to.[29]

In marriage, a man and a woman are united so
they become one flesh in sexual union.[30] The common
aim of marriage is procreation, creating a family, and the
ripening of a relationship between two people.[31] These
purposes for marriage move towards love and away from
treating a person as the means to end.[32]

Sexual relationships can lead to merely using
another person not as a subject but an object.[33] Another
person should not be used as a source of sexual
pleasure.[34] Enjoyment of another must always be
subordinate to love.[35]

All human beings are by nature sexual beings and
are born male or female.[36] The attributes of man and
woman are complementary so that man and woman can
complete each other.[37]

The normal form of sexual desire in people is
directed towards another human being.[38] If it is directed
towards the sexual attributes of another, it is an

---

[28] Ibid.
[29] Ibid, p. 29.
[30] Ibid, p. 30.
[31] Ibid.
[32] Ibid.
[33] Ibid.
[34] Ibid, p. 34.
[35] Ibid.
[36] Ibid, p. 47.
[37] Ibid, p. 48.
[38] Ibid, p. 49.

impoverishment and a perversion of the desire.[39] In many ways our culture is full of such sexual perversion. For example, consider the obsession with women's breasts. Sexual desire towards a sexual body part not a whole person is a perversion.

Love is not merely a biological or psychological manifestation of sexual desire.[40] Love grows out of sexual desire and develops and takes shape by acts of will by the person.[41] Sexual desire plays a part in the divine order.[42] It is a form of participation in the work of creation – procreation.[43]

Love is a mutual relationship between two people.[44] It involves attraction but it is not just attraction.[45] Love is the fullest realization of the possibility in the human being.[46] It is a reciprocal, mutual friendship. Betrothed love is the giving of ones own person to another.[47] Each surrenders to the other[48] and it must be a full giving of the entire person not just giving sexually.[49] Each must see the value of the person and value the person first as a person and only second as a sexual being.[50]

---

[39] Ibid.
[40] Ibid.
[41] Ibid.
[42] Ibid, p. 62.
[43] Ibid.
[44] Ibid, p. 73.
[45] Ibid, p. 76.
[46] Ibid, p. 82.
[47] Ibid, p. 96.
[48] Ibid, p. 98.
[49] Ibid, p. 99.
[50] Ibid, p. 122.

In love there is responsibility.[51] The greater the feeling of responsibility for another person, the greater the true love there is.[52] We love the person with all their virtues and faults - independent of their virtues and in spite of their faults.[53] The strength of that love shows clearly when the beloved person stumbles.[54] One who truly loves does not withdraw when seeing weakness but loves more.[55] A person never loses his or her essential value.[56]

Humility is the proper attitude towards all true greatness, including one's own greatness, but above all towards the greatest outside one's self.[57] The human body must humble itself, subordinate itself in the face of love.[58] Chastity helps with this. In the absence of chastity the body is not subordinated to love.[59]

As you move towards marriage, begin to think about what you have learned in this chapter. Are you subordinating yourself to God? Are you using others for your sexual pleasure to the detriment of seeing another's greatness and treating that greatest appropriately? Are you practicing chastity if you are single?

---

[51] Ibid, p. 130.
[52] Ibid., p. 131.
[53] Ibid, p. 135.
[54] Ibid.
[55] Ibid.
[56] Ibid.
[57] Ibid, p. 172.
[58] Ibid.
[59] Ibid.

Understanding why God created marriage will help you put your own desires about marriage into a bigger and greater context – the context of our Lord.

Find the right husband for you
(any old husband will not do)

<u>What is a husband?</u>

Proverbs 31, The Ideal Wife[60], is not usually used to explore what the ideal husband is.[61] However, this passage, and the entire Book of Proverbs, was really addressed to men.[62] A woman that lived in ancient times would not have had the kind of freedom and responsibility described without the support and encouragement of her husband.[63] The woman's character as a godly woman is directly related to close relationship with God.[64] However, the freedom she had was most likely made possible by her husband.[65]

<u>What are the attributes of the ideal husband?</u>

- He truly appreciates his wife
- He has complete confidence in his wife's faithfulness
- He has faith in his wife's abilities as manager and gives her the freedom to function

---

[60] This passage is printed in full in the "How To Be A Good Wife" chapter.
[61] "A Model for Marriage," Bob Deffinbaugh, www.bible.org , 09-08-09.
[62] Ibid.
[63] Ibid.
[64] Ibid.
[65] Ibid.

- He appreciates her value and gives her the praise she deserves

Some husbands restrict their wives from fully utilizing their gifts and abilities because they are threatened by their wife's competence.[66] Proverbs 31 teaches us that the ideal wife has much more freedom than most husbands are willing to grant.[67] Husbands need to recognize that in their role as managers, they need to utilize the abilities of their wives to the fullest degree.[68]

Proverbs 31 points out that the ideal wife does nearly everything her husband does, including tasks that were considered masculine such as earning income, being in the business world, and being a manager. [69] The main difference between husbands and wives, is not that some things are male and some are female.[70] The difference is that wives act under the authority of their husbands.[71] She has great freedom and authority, but it is within the confines of the authority of her husband, the head of the household.[72]

This might be difficult for some people to hear. I used to want everything completely equal and did not want to subordinate myself to anyone, including God. As I have grown in my faith, I now see that to allow my

---

[66] Ibid.
[67] Ibid.
[68] Ibid.
[69] Ibid.
[70] Ibid.
[71] Ibid.
[72] Ibid.

husband to be the head of the household does not take anything away from me as a wife. My husband respects me, honors me, cherishes me, and knows that I am a smart and capable person. We make major decisions together. He requests my counsel and listens to me. In addition, he leaves many things to me to decide.

Christ is our head, but we have a great deal of freedom and responsibility.[73] Wives should feel no more stifled under the leadership of their husbands than we do under the headship of Christ.[74]

That brings us to a more common and traditional Bible passage that is used to describe and define husbands:

Husbands, love your wives, just as Christ loved the church and gave himself up for her to make her holy, cleansing her by the washing with water through the word, and to present her to himself as a radiant church, without stain or wrinkle or any other blemish, but holy and blameless. In this same way, husbands ought to love their wives as their own bodies. He who loves his wife loves himself. After all, no one ever hated his own body, but he feeds and cares for it, just as Christ does the church—for we are members of his body. "For this reason a man will leave his father and mother and be united to his wife, and the two will become one flesh." This is a profound mystery—but I am talking about Christ and the church. However, each one of you also must love

---

[73] Ibid.
[74] Ibid.

his wife as he loves himself, and the wife must respect her husband.

The love a husband should have for his wife is a holy love that cleanses and lifts up. Husbands should love their wives as they love themselves, for indeed the husband and wife are one under God. Husbands leave their parents and become one with their wives, thus creating a new primary family.

Your husband should complement you. (He should compliment you too!). As individuals we have shortcomings and weaknesses. Part of the beauty of marriage is that you get to join yourself with another person. Although you still will not be a perfect couple, hopefully where one is weak the other will be strong, or at least stronger.

Your husband should be a man who is worthy of you. He should make you a better and stronger woman. My husband met me as I was. He saw my strengths and weaknesses and was honest with me about them. He pushed, and continues to push me, to become the woman I was destined to be. Because of him, and God, I am stronger, wiser, more confident, and happier.

I've had friends that used a checklist of traits (rich, intelligent, funny, handsome, athletic, etc.) to find a mate. When I was dating my husband, I used a list of topics to discuss that I believe is more appropriate and will prove to be fruitful. Please note that this is not an exhaustive list. Please add other things that are important to you.

Exercise - Topics to Discuss With a Suitor

1. Religion/Spirituality
2. Children
3. Family
4. Marriage
5. Sexuality
6. Work
7. Money
8. Housework
9. Divorce
10. Education
11. History/Past
12. Friends
13. Food
14. Health
15. Exercise
16. Relationships
17. Addictions
18. Hobbies
19. Travel
20. Home (where to live/type of house)
21. Dreams
22. Fears

A list like this helps you to learn more about yourself and each other, and helps you determine how compatible you are. I used this with my husband and we had lots of fun each night on the phone discussing these things!

How to be a good wife

He who finds a wife finds what is good and receives favor from the LORD.

Proverbs 18:22

Before we look at the model wife, let's look at the model woman. For many, Miss America is a model woman.[75] The ideal woman is seen as young, single, and sexy.[76] The ideal woman we find in Proverbs 31 is very different.[77]

The sayings of King Lemuel—an oracle his mother taught him:

O my son, O son of my womb, O son of my vows,

Do not spend your strength on women, your vigor on those who ruin kings.

"It is not for kings, O Lemuel— not for kings to drink wine, not for rulers to crave beer,

Lest they drink and forget what the law decrees, and deprive all the oppressed of their rights.

---

[75] "A Model for Marriage," Bob Deffinbaugh, www.bible.org, 09-08-09.
[76] Ibid.
[77] Ibid.

Give beer to those who are perishing, wine to those who are in anguish;

Let them drink and forget their poverty and remember their misery no more.

"Speak up for those who cannot speak for themselves, for the rights of all who are destitute.

Speak up and judge fairly; defend the rights of the poor and needy."
   Epilogue: The Wife of Noble Character

A wife of noble character who can find? She is worth far more than rubies.

Her husband has full confidence in her and lacks nothing of value.

She brings him good, not harm, all the days of her life.

She selects wool and flax and works with eager hands.

She is like the merchant ships, bringing her food from afar.

She gets up while it is still dark; she provides food for her family and portions for her servant girls.

She considers a field and buys it; out of her earnings she plants a vineyard.

She sets about her work vigorously; her arms are strong for her tasks.

She sees that her trading is profitable, and her lamp does not go out at night.

In her hand she holds the distaff and grasps the spindle with her fingers.

She opens her arms to the poor and extends her hands to the needy.

When it snows, she has no fear for her household; for all of them are clothed in scarlet.

She makes coverings for her bed; she is clothed in fine linen and purple.

Her husband is respected at the city gate, where he takes his seat among the elders of the land.

She makes linen garments and sells them, and supplies the merchants with sashes.

She is clothed with strength and dignity; she can laugh at the days to come.

She speaks with wisdom, and faithful instruction is on her tongue.

She watches over the affairs of her household and does not eat the bread of idleness.

*Her children arise and call her blessed; her husband
also, and he praises her:*

"Many women do noble things, but you surpass them all."

*Charm is deceptive, and beauty is fleeting; but a woman
who fears the LORD is to be praised.*

*Give her the reward she has earned, and let her works
bring her praise at the city gate.*

Proverbs 31

The ideal woman is a married woman but we
don't know her age or whether she is physically
attractive.[78] Her most important quality is her
godliness.[79] The woman of Proverbs 31 is almost perfect.
She works incredibly hard, is extremely competent and
compassionate.[80] She represents an almost impossible
standard.[81] The title of Proverbs 31 is The Ideal Wife and
she is a model to be imitated even though it may be hard
to reach the ideal.[82]

In many ways, this passage was written more to
help men to be better husbands than it was to help women
become better wives.[83] (See my chapter "Find the Right

---

[78] Ibid.
[79] Ibid.
[80] Ibid.
[81] Ibid.
[82] Ibid.
[83] Ibid.

Husband for You.") There is a lesson for both husbands and wives, not only about the character of the godly wife, but also about the responsibility of the godly husband to help his wife to reach her full potential as a wife.[84]

What are the qualities of the ideal wife?

- She has unusual character
- She is completely trustworthy
- She is hard-working
- She is wise
- She is generous
- She instructs in a gentle way[85]

What are the responsibilities of the Ideal Wife?

- Purchasing agent for family
- Manager
- Provider of income
- Investor
- Producer
- Giver to the poor
- Teacher

---

[84] Ibid.
[85] Ibid.

- Promoter of her husband's standing and leadership in the community

An important principle underlying this passage is that the efforts of the wife should contribute to the well-being of the family.[86]

What kind of wife will you be? I think of the blessed virgin, Mary, when I think of the model woman, wife and mother. Just look at a statue of her and you will be reminded of some of her qualities. She is fully clothed with modest, loose free-flowing garments. Her hands are outstretched showing how giving, generous, kind and loving she is. She is peaceful and calm. Reserved and pleasant. She is humbled and unadorned with no jewelry or make-up. She is confident and completely balanced because she has turned over her life to God's will with willingness and acceptance. This is the kind of woman I strive to be and I ask Mary, to pray for me to be a good wife and mother.

One great thing about not having yet found your husband is that you get to keep working on yourself as you are, and keep learning about how to be a good woman, wife, and mother. That way, if and when you meet him, you will be more prepared to be a good wife.

---

[86] Ibid.

Looking for love in all the right places

There are so many places to meet the right person. I won't say that there are any wrong places but I do know that some locales are overrated and might not come through for you. The first such places that come to mind are nightclubs and bars. I used to go to clubs when I was younger. The combination of loud suggestive music, provocative dressing, alcohol and drugs, and dark lights do not make it a wholesome place to meet people. I no longer go to bars, but, when I see them on television now, they look to me like a glimpse of hell. Needless to say, they are probably not the place to meet the love of your life.

Nevertheless, you could meet the right person just about anywhere: the grocery store, a park, church, bookstore, or car wash. Wherever there are people. The Lord works in mysterious ways. If God wants you to meet someone, you will meet them! The key is being open to love – God's love.

I think it is both about being open to God and about opening your eyes to see the right things. For example, if you are fixated on looks, think of all the people that are beautiful on the inside that you will overlook. Have you ever met an attractive person and then once you saw their unattractive personality they actually began to look unattractive to you? It is the same in reverse. A physically unattractive person at first glance can appear beautiful even physically if you like or love them.

There is a famous story of a man who searched and searched for diamonds and never found them. After his death, they found diamonds in his very backyard! For us, it might not be that we are looking in the wrong place but that we are not looking for the right things.

There are several online dating services with a spiritual or religious focus. Try them out. There are Catholic, Christian and Jewish sites. These are good because they put God back into the selection of a mate.

Home is where the heart is

"From every human being there rises a light that reaches straight to heaven, and when two souls that are designed to be together find each other, their streams of light flow together and a single, brighter light goes forth from their united being."

Author Unknown

How will you know when you have met "the one." Many say it feels like you are finally home. That's the way it felt for me. It doesn't mean it is perfect. It wasn't for me and it probably won't be for you. But home isn't perfect either. There's dust and dirty laundry. But home is comfortable, it fits and it makes you feel like you belong. Once again I will direct you back to prayer. You will need to be in constant communication with God. Talking to God, or praying, is how you will know that you are on the right track.

Home is also the place where your marriage will live! You make a home. Home is a place where a person feels welcome. Where they feel love. And where they always know they can return to. What is your home like? Is it comfortable and beautiful? Do you spend time making it feel like home? Do you spend time there? If you marry, you and your husband will be creating a home together. Think about yourself as a home-maker and cultivating a peaceful home. Practice staying home and enjoying it! There should be a healthy balance between being home and being out. If you don't like being home, ask yourself and God why. I have family and friends that are never home. And many of them do not seem very happy. I think there might be a connection. I love being home. I love making our home a clean, comfortable and beautiful place for my husband and son.

Make a great home for yourself. When and if you meet the right one, invite him in!

Divorce should not be an option

Marriage vows are a solemn promise before God. The love between a husband and wife is symbolic of God's love and God's love is forever. That's the way marriage is supposed to be – forever. I firmly believe that many people don't enter into marriage with a clear idea of what they want. Many people don't see marriage as permanent and therefore they don't make a permanent lifelong commitment. They might say they do, but they don't in their hearts.

I come from a history of divorce. My mother and father got divorced. My grandmother and grandfather on both sides got divorced. My mother remarried and got divorced again. I know this influenced me to not believe in or trust marriage.

The best way to prevent a divorce is to not believe in it. If you simply do not consider divorce to be an option, when times get rough you don't even think about going down that road. It goes back to the definition of marriage as two people being joined into one by God. Forever. Period. It doesn't get any easier than that conceptually. Marriage is not always easy. But neither is life. We can't just quit life when it gets hard.

Some dear people in my life were having marital problems. They were thinking of divorce. Not planning divorce but keeping it in mind as an option. That was the worst thing they could do if they wanted their marriage to work. In order to make their marriage work and last, they had to give up the option of divorce.

My husband tells me all the time "I will never leave you." I tell him the same thing. When I tell him I will never leave him it is because I see our marriage as between him, me and God, and I can never leave God. When I get terribly mad at my husband, I never bring up divorce. I honestly do not believe in divorce. I am married for life.

The power of prayer, faith and belief

THE 23RD PSALM

The Lord is my shepherd; I shall not want.

He maketh me to lie down in green pastures: he leadeth me beside the still waters.

He restoreth my soul: he leadeth me in the paths of righteousness for his name's sake.

Yea, though I walk through the valley of the shadow of death, I will fear no evil: for thou art with me; thy rod and thy staff they comfort me.

Thou preparest a table before me in the presence of mine enemies: thou anointest my head with oil; my cup runneth over.

Surely goodness and mercy shall follow me all the days of my life: and I will dwell in the house of the Lord for ever.

It is completely essential that we have prayer and a personal relationship with God. Prayer is spiritual food. We need it for our sprits to thrive. It is remarkable what prayer can do. It makes us closer to God. It reminds us who is in charge, God. It puts into perspective our relationship with God. It reminds us that God protects and guides us. It allows us to give up our worry and anxiety and turn them over to God. And it allows us to give God thanks and praise for all that he has done for us. To be fully joyful and grateful.

Some times we want something so badly that we overlook the negative and don't listen to the voice of God. Please keep an open dialog with God. Follow the Holy Spirit. Listen more and talk less.

Trust in the Lord with all your heart and do not lean on your own understanding. In all your ways acknowledge Him, and He will make your paths straight.

Proverbs 3:5-6

May God Bless You

Follow your dreams. Don't give up. You can have a happy and fulfilling life with or without a husband. But I hope it is God's will for you to have a husband because they are pretty great. I love mine and wouldn't trade him for all the tea in China![87] May God bless you always!

---

[87] My husband tells me this all the time!

Bibliography

"A Guideline for Writing the Story of Your Marriage." *Archdiocese of Washington*. June 2005. Web.

Deaton, Cathy. "Fire is the Test of Gold - There is No Perfection Without Refinement." *Ezinearticles.com*. Web. 13 Sept. 2009.

Deffinbaugh, Bob. "A Model for Marriage." *Bible.org*. Web. 8 Sept. 2009.

Keller, W. Phillip. A Shepherd Looks at Psalm 23. Grand Rapids, MI: Zondervan, 2007.

"Marriage Matters." *Archdiocese of Washington*. Web. Sept. 2009.

Singletary, Michelle. The Power to Prosper: 21 Days to Financial Freedom. Grand Rapids, MI: Zondervan, 2010.

Stanley, Charles. "The Desires of the Heart." *In Touch Ministries*. Dr. Charles Stanley. Web. 13 Sept. 2009.

Stanley, Charles. "Landmines in the Path of the Believer, Part 5: The Landmine of Sexual Sins." *In Touch Ministries*. Dr. Charles Stanley. Web. 13 Sept. 2009.

West, Christopher. *The Theology of the Body.net*. Christopher West. Web. 26 Sept. 2009.

Wojtyla, Karol (Pope John Paul II). Love and
Responsibility. Trans. H.T. Willetts. San Francisco, CA:
Ignatius Press, 1981.

Proof

Made in the USA
Charleston, SC
02 March 2010